Easy words to read

Hen's pens

...bee Cox

...phen Cartwright

...nny Tyler

...onsultant:

...Grant

...hD, AFBPs, CPsychol

There is a yellow duck to find on every page.

First published in 2001 by Usborne Publishing Ltd. Usborne House, 83-85 Saffron Hill, London EC1N 8RT, England. www.usborne.com
Copyright © 2001 Usborne Publishing Ltd.

Hen has new pens.

She has ten
new pens.

3

"When will you use your new pens, Hen?"

"Now, Brown Cow!"

"What will you draw?"

"Straw...

5

... and the big blue sky,
and a yellow bird flying by."

Hen hops
off her
nest.

"Drawing patterns is
what I like best."

7

She zigs and zags from left to right.

"Draw big dots on your eggs."
"Or more zigzags?" Hen begs.

Hen's zigzags are very bright indeed.

"Zigzags are just what ALL eggs need!"

...if I zigzag
all the eggs
I find."

Now everyone's eggs are in a dreadful mix.

14

"I'm sure the others will not mind...

Sorting them out
is hard to fix.

Hen has made a bad mistake.
That's not her chick.

It's a baby snake!